About the

I inherited my love of animals from my Aunt Amy, who I later found out, was my birth mother.

Initially I was considering a career in journalism, but family events took over so that did not materialise. I felt drawn to rural life with animals soon after meeting my husband and began breeding and showing American Quarter Horses. After that, Cotswold sheep became my focus and once again I bred and showed them with success.

The decision in 1991 to move to Herefordshire and begin renovating an old cottage with land resulted in me selling my flock, replacing it with ducks, aka *Puddles and Pals*.

A near fatal car crash in 2005 has slowed me up somewhat, but my love of country life, my dogs, ducks and also my cottage garden remains strong. It is my way of life. I love it.

PUDDLES AND PALS

Marion L Stapleton Harley

PUDDLES AND PALS

Vanguard Press

VANGUARD PAPERBACK

A CIP catalogue record for this title is
available from the British Library.

ISBN 978 1 784659 62 2

Vanguard Press is an imprint of
Pegasus Elliot MacKenzie Publishers Ltd.
www.pegasuspublishers.com

First Published in 2021

Vanguard Press
Sheraton House Castle Park
Cambridge England

Printed and Bound in Great Britain

Dedication

I could list several people. Those who helped in so many ways. Those who have travelled with me down many tracks and lanes. Those who have made it possible.

So as not to offend any, by reason of position in the list, I choose those without whom there would be no book.

Dedicated to my Jack Russells and my ducks.

To everyone else, a heartfelt, thank you.

Puddles and Pals

Moby Duck, one of my Indian Runner drakes—
Indian Runners look like wine bottles on legs and
they do run. When I did my research about ducks,
it included researching names. I saw 'Moby Duck'
listed and that was it… I just had to have a drake
so I could use the name. So pleased I did. Moby
has become a feathered friend.

My tale began December 2015 when I opened my Christmas stocking and found a box of duck eggs. The words 'Braddock Whites' were emblazoned on the lid. Six gleaming white large eggs. Having kept ducks in the past and inspired by my Christmas eggs, I decided to track down Braddock Whites and revive my duck keeping of years past. I like ducks and find their eggs really tasty. I have many allergies and get on better with duck eggs than hen, so that gave me further encouragement.

My husband was not averse to the idea, so my hunt for Braddock Whites began. The obvious starting point was where my eggs came from — the farm, not Waitrose. I contacted them easily enough but was informed that they did not sell live ducks. Undeterred, I looked up Braddock Whites on my mobile.

No computer access where we live and mobile use can be 'iffy'. Oddly enough no information showed when I trawled through breeds of ducks. All the usual and the unusual, but no Braddock Whites. I rang the British Waterfowl Association but they knew of no such breed. However, they kindly offered to make enquiries on my behalf and a few days later an email arrived with news of Braddock Whites — there is no such breed. However, the B.W.A. had been in contact with breeders of ducks and the general opinion was that my Braddock Whites eggs were laid by Cherry

Valley ducks — a large commercial duck of Pekin/Aylesbury origin.

Further investigation via my mobile was called for and there was a lot of duck talk.

Coincidentally, around this time, a newly-acquired friend gave me a box of duck eggs. Not large white ones but beautiful large greeny blue eggs. No need for detailed search for the breed this time — I simply asked my friend — Indian Runners. I am well-acquainted with the I. R. — a leading keeper of fowl in the Cotswolds once described them as "a Hock bottle on legs". I'd always thought that phrase extremely accurate and found their characteristic odd stance and waddle both amusing and endearing.

For several days I thought duck, talked duck and ate my way through duck — eggs, that is. My decision was made. I would have Indian Runners and one Cherry Valley — after all it was their eggs that started the whole thing even if they were sold under the code name Braddock Whites.

Searching for a reputable source from where to obtain my baby ducks turned out to be relatively straightforward. One of the contacts made by the B.W.A. lived near Bristol — not a few miles away, but Bristol... and she had both Indian Runners and Cherry Valley. Few things are initially as simple as first thought and it was a while before I was able to make the car journey with a friend to collect my baby ducks. Due to a satnav error we travelled the scenic route but it was a really pretty journey and much nicer than motorway or 'A' roads. Indeed, some of the lanes we travelled had grass growing in the middle — even long enough to cut in some places.

We duly arrived and behind a lovely old rectory in the back of beyond, was the barn, where inside I would find my goal — my ducklings. The breeder had seemed very knowledgeable and friendly via emails and she was in person. I had previously decided to have five trout-coloured Indian Runners, four would suffice, but I'd get five — just in case, plus my one Cherry Valley. So, six one-week-old baby ducks would travel home with us. Actually seven made the return journey. I'd spent some time researching duck names and found some great ones. I thought 'Moby Duck' was brilliant. I could not give that name to a girl duck and so duck number seven is a white Indian Runner drake — Moby Duck. I didn't want him to feel the odd one out, colourwise, so I had one white Indian Runner and four trout females.

I'd allocated 'Puddles' as the name for my Cherry Valley. My husband had been suggesting names, most of which I discarded, but his Mrs. Whippy for my white Indian Runner, as in Mr. Whippy ice cream, the connection being both are white, had stayed in my mind. I wasn't too keen on the 'Mrs' bit and trimmed it down to 'Whippy'. So, Puddles, Moby Duck, Whippy and Nibbles — his character developed early — began their lives in a converted rabbit hutch in our study.

The name plaque on their duck house reads 'Puddles and Pals'. I will need to find three more suitable names, which could take some time. I am very grateful to my husband who has built them the perfect duck house and to friends who have helped me in getting project 'Duck' started. The purpose is mainly for us to have home-laid, free range duck eggs for personal use. However, having six future egg-laying ducks will probably mean quite a surplus of eggs. If anyone would like to buy some beautiful greeny-blue or gleaming white duck eggs, please get in touch! There will be a little wait until eggs are available but it will be worth it.

So, I now have my own flock!

'Puddles and Pals' — my seven ducks... one drake and six ducks for egg laying.

They were all safely transferred to their duck house on 1st June. All very satisfactory and an old radio gave them some entertainment for the first few days whilst they adjusted to the new routine. When I'm doing the gardening, no radio is needed, as they observe me with great interest, quacking with gusto, keeping an eye on what I'm doing and where I'm doing it.

There are two large linked pens on the lawn,

into which they are transported daily. Please take 'transported' in the literal sense. An old electric mower, no longer cutting well, is the transporter base and a small dog pen sits on top… thanks again to my carpenter husband and his many skills. The 'duck trolley', as I call it, is put near the Duck House pophole door, a cute little ramp (more thanks to my husband) goes in between and the door is raised. There are sides to the ramp to ensure they actually go into the pen rather than escape into the garden. The excited quacking ceases, a head pops out — usually Puddles — who rotates her head and eyes, weighing up the situation. Up the ramp she goes into the pen, followed by the others with varying degrees of speed. 1, 2, 3, 4, 5, 6… 6,6,6,? It has to be Nibbles left behind and her bill is just visible through the door as I say encouraging words. The decision made, out she comes, up the ramp she goes, but can't get into the pen as the others, fed up of waiting have decided to exit and we are all back where we started. A quick duck conference and all seven troop up the ramp into the pen which I rapidly close.

I have always talked to my dogs who I know, without doubt, understand a lot of what I say (this has been proved to interested persons — doubters and believers alike) and so I see no reason not to talk to my ducks. Most animals like a routine and respond to chat, thus they become tame and easier to handle. Well — that is my theory.

"Health and Safety,"' I explain to them as I check the pen is secure and away we go to the two large pens on the lawn.

Reversing the procedure for disembarkation they come tumbling out, down the ramp into the pen and head for the duck bath. Actually, it is a plastic dog basket, filled with water, but it does the job.

When I feed them — twice daily —I always say 'lunch'… 'early lunch' is breakfast and 'late lunch' indicates teatime. At bedtime the entire routine is reversed and they happily return to the Duck House for the night.

Indian Runners do not fly — or so my research indicated. One late afternoon having made the return trip to the Duck House, I opened the trolley pen door. 'Puddles' followed by a couple of trout Indian Runners disembarked, 'Moby Duck' was next, but halfway down the ramp, flapping his wings violently, he slowly rose into the air and glided with great grace over the ramp sides and gently came to rest on the lawn. The remaining occupants of the duck trolley pen had by now gone into the Duck House so I moved the ramp and guided Moby in. I think he was as surprised as me by what had occurred and seemed happy to join his friends.

My husband's next task was to increase the height of the ramp sides and thus avoid any more flying experiences!

A few weeks passed and I made a rash decision one late afternoon, to let them out of the lawn enclosure to make their own way back to the Duck House. A great success — and now this is part of the daily routine. They enjoy several hours on what used to be our lawn (it now resembles a well-used football pitch) before loud quacking lets me know they want to go to bed.

As I was admiring them one sunny afternoon, looking at the distinctive tail feathers of my drake, Moby, I realised it was not Moby, as the person from whom I bought them, makes a notch on the foot of all the drakes when hatched. The white duck in front of me had curled tail feathers as all drakes do, but did not have a notched foot! My little flock of laying ducks would be reduced to five and I would be unable to breed white Indian Runners.

Several emails were exchanged between me and the breeder near Bristol, ending with her kindly saying she would let me have a white Indian Runner duck (girl) free of charge. She had offered to exchange 'Whippy' (who was initially presumed to be a duck but turned out to be the second drake) but I just could not do that. The situation was not his fault... he had been with me and the others since he was one week of age, he'd had swimming lessons in the bath, navigated the ramp with ease and was happy with life here. How could I remove him from his friends? I also felt there was the possibility that he could go the same way as cockerels when too many are around.

So, off to Bristol again for one white Indian Runner duck (girl). The same good friend who had come with me on the first trip, gallantly said she would come along for the second. Darth Vader — the voice on my satnav — had not been previously 100% reliable and as my friend has the ability to read road maps (I can also do that) whilst going along (I can't do that) we set off with confidence. Sure enough, the map was read perfectly and we arrived at the poultry place without mishap. We did approach it from the other direction than before and had to ask for final run-in directions —

it is in the back of beyond — but arrived full of enthusiasm to collect the new duck.

For those of you who recall the first part of Puddles and Pals, you may recall I needed three more names.

Puddles, Moby Duck, Whippy and Nibbles had been allocated and a short time later, Pod, Waddles and Ziggy were added to the name board. There was not much room to write another as no further addition had been expected. As I contemplated various names and wondered how I could fit it onto the bottom of the board, I thought to myself, 'this has thrown a spanner in the works. Job done... 'Spanner' has settled in very well with her new friends.

The 26th September was a great day. I opened up the Duck House at 7am and there, laying resplendent on the straw, was my first egg. I ate it for lunch... wonderful!

My little flock of ducks is thriving. The six ducks and two drakes have settled into the daily routine of travelling in their trolley pen to the relevant enclosure, then roaming around the gardens until their bedtime. I would say they are now highly trained. However, my husband may disagree.

Late November 2016 saw me handing over full duck care to him. No option as major foot surgery meant I couldn't leave our cottage for many weeks and unable to negotiate our sloping lawn for months. He did his best but the ducks were used to my voice. At teatime I used to call "wheat treat " and they would all come running. All except Puddles who waddles rather than runs. As one of my Indian Runners is actually named Waddles it is now obvious that Puddles should have been named Waddles and Waddles... Puddles... if you follow the flow. Anyway, .me calling, "wheat treat" results in them all arriving at the large glass bowl filled with fresh water, into which I throw scoops of wheat. They love it. Feet and feathers mingle whilst they clamber around, dipping their heads and necks into the water to devour the sunken wheat. My husband, saying wheat treat failed to have the same effect for a while, but in the end, a compromise was reached between them and whilst not racing to get to the bowl they did amble across. Over the next few weeks, their speed gradually increased and I have to admit that after a while, him calling "wheat treat " had a similar effect as when I did.

Seeing my ducks pottering around outside whilst I was confined indoors, unable to care for them, was not good. However, needs must and he obviously looked after them to a good standard as egg laying was excellent. The flavour is wonderful and duck eggs suit me perfectly. Having many food allergies, I get on far better with duck eggs than chicken eggs. Eggs are good for dogs as well and our two Jack Russells love breakfast when it is a boiled egg day.

I am now at the stage in my convalescence when I can get out of the cottage and once again look after my ducks myself… well, most of the time. When taking back control a few weeks ago, I thought it would work well if the ducks were allowed to roam the gardens freely. It would mean that I couldn't let the dogs out, but I felt sure that problem could be overcome.

Our Jack Russells have been wonderful company for me, especially during the time when I was confined to remaining indoors. They stayed with me throughout. I am sure the dog owners among you will understand how the company of a dog can lift one's spirits through difficult times. So, as soon as I was able, I decided to put the new plan into action. I managed to stagger down the lawn and let the ducks out.

The only resulting problem was that I couldn't let the Jack Russells out to free range. Free-range ducks and free-range Jack Russells do not mix. As my mobility improved, I thought I'd solve the problem by taking out the Jack Russells individually on their harness and lead. The ducks would not become lunch for the dogs and the dogs could stretch their legs without problems... or so I thought.

The time came... ducks roaming free in the gardens and one Jack Russell ready to exit the front door with me for a gentle stroll along the path. Neither I nor dog was expecting what followed. I'd seen that all eight ducks were right down the bottom of the garden happily pottering in our Conservation Patch. I opened the door and carefully exited the cottage with a happy and calm Jack Russell. We descended the front step and began to slowly proceed along the path. That scenario did not last long. Before we had taken only a few paces, the two drakes — Moby (Duck) and Whippy had left the grazing ducks down the bottom and raced up the garden. Up the lawn at great speed they came, through the flower beds, ending up eye-to-eye with my bewildered Jack Russell. I had no idea what would happen next.

The Jack Russell with me can give a good impression of the Tasmanian Devil in seconds and my lack of mobility was a major problem. We managed to beat a retreat into the cottage and consider the next move.

I hoisted myself back up the step with my Jack Russell — his ears flat and looking somewhat perturbed. Once back inside I gave the problem serious thought. I had to be able to get the dogs out somehow. Cautiously and as quietly as I could, I once again opened the door. We never got off the step at all this time another retreat into the cottage.

At this point I was sure I could out think a couple of drakes. A cunning plan was required I, with dog, would exit out the side door at the end of the cottage into an area the ducks have so far not found. It is completely out of sight from the bottom of the garden and should suit the purpose perfectly. I carefully opened the door.

Well — that was it — both dogs imprisoned in our cottage by two drakes, Moby Duck and Whippy.

I had tried to smuggle ourselves out through the door but before you could say, "We've made it," Moby and Whippy appeared around the corner at great speed. Moby in the lead — he always is. I have no idea how they knew we were there but they did. Another retreat. Nature's needs must so about half an hour later I tried again. This time I encouraged my Jack Russell to turn right up a little bank towards the little wicket gate and at last success... he had a wee. I tried the same method with his son, our smaller Jack Russell, but he was stubborn — more or less curling himself up into a ball rather than put one foot in front of the other. Obviously, the success achieved with his father was not going to be repeated with stubborn son. No undignified clambering up a bank for him.

I was sure he needed a wee so decided a face-to-bill confrontation could not be avoided. I opened the front door quietly and we set off. Hadn't got off the front step before both drakes were there. Eyes-to-eyes as they looked him in the face. I endeavoured to keep them from nudging him around and we slowly made our way along the path with my Jack Russell looking very wary. Me managing to keep my balance and remain more or less upright with Jack Russell junior keeping close to my leg staring straight ahead, both of us escorted by a drake on each side.

One would have thought the four of us had practised for hours. Paws and feet seemingly in perfect time. We arrived at the wire gate, which opens onto our car park area, with everyone intact and I managed to get myself and dog through without the company of our escorts. Moby and Whippy stood on the path looking through like two sentries on guard. Jack Russell junior had his wee and the process was repeated in reverse and we returned to the safety of the cottage. Once through the door, our escorts deviated off back over the flower bed and down to where the girl ducks had been happily pottering, seemingly oblivious to the scenes of male chivalry which had played out in earnest. All none the worse for the experience.

Seeing that the Jack Russells have become involved with Puddles and Pals and there is a remote possibility that they may become pals of Puddles etc., it is only fair that their names should be made known in case they are included in further tales: Cadfael (as in Brother) and his son Cider… so named as the mother of Cadfael was named Scrumpy. Cider is also often referred to as The Urchin… but that is another tale.

The whole lengthy procedures of getting the dogs outside had exhausted me as, apart from lacking energy, my balance and ability to walk was not up to much. I would not be able to continue with this method for the weeks of convalescence that lay ahead.

An even more cunning plan would be required for the future…

A great deal of thought was required. Knowing that food can often be an incentive, I considered the possibility of somehow bringing it into the equation. It would not be possible for me to go outside to lay a trap but I definitely felt it could somehow solve the problem.

Oh joy! I was right. Wheat was the solution. I would balance by the front door and throw the wheat as far as possible, a bit like throwing rice at a wedding.

The ducks would be pottering down the bottom of the garden, whilst it rained wheat grains nearby. Whilst they ferreted around, their bills working vigorously to pick up the tasty treat, I would manoeuvre myself off the step clutching a lead. On the other end was a Jack Russell — whichever one had the most need. We would work our way along the path until reaching the safety of our car park area. Once there, we could relax for a short while — albeit a very short while — as it never took Moby and his second in command Whippy, very long to sense that a Jack Russell had escaped from the cottage and should be challenged. They would leave the girl ducks and run up the lawn as fast as possible to try and attack before the return journey had been completed.

Indian Runners do actually run. They tend to look like wine bottles on legs, but when racing along with the intent of attacking something, they lower their heads, their beaks protruding forward like missiles waiting to be launched.

So for several weeks, the regular trips to the car park area were fraught with tension. One would never have thought that two drakes could cause so much humiliation to two Jack Russells — a breed well known for being fearless in most situations.

I am sure that many interesting scenarios lie ahead with my project 'Duck'.

I would incubate some of the eggs and hatch baby quacks. I would also resolve the issue of ducks versus dogs. Further tales of feathers and fur await.

Fun and Games

'The boys': Cadfael and Cider, father and son. Jack Russells are intelligent, vocal, determined, energetic and fearless, as well as very loving and affectionate. It is quite normal when passing others for serious growls to be heard, followed by knowing looks between owners.

My two Jack Russells are a very important part of the family: Cadfael and Cider, father and son.

Cadfael has whingeing down to a fine art. If it was an Olympic sport, our cottage walls would be adorned with medals suspended from brightly coloured ribbons. Indeed, I would go further, he has developed it into more than a fine art... he has invented a language. The language of 'Whinge'. He speaks, I listen and know exactly what he is saying... or to be more accurate, what he wants.

It consists of a variety of tones, almost an octave to be precise, and the length of each tone conveying to the listener, an accurate translation of what he wants. As far as he is concerned, he'll say it once and expect results. I keep surprising myself at how well I understand Whinge. I seem to be the only one who does. To be fair, my husband and I are the only two permanently living in our cottage and as such the most exposed to Whinge. Nevertheless, whilst I have been the perfect student and have immediate understanding of Cadfael's requirements, he has not. I could expand on the reasons for this failure, but feel most of you reading this, will be nodding with complete understanding. Whinge does have its uses, for both Cadfael and for me.

Cadfael and Cider each have a good-sized pen in our bedroom where they sleep. I am aware that not all dog owners would want this, but in my situation, it works very well. There is plenty of space and Cadfael's pen is nearest to the headboard end of our bed, with Cider, aka 'The Urchin' next to him.

Due to my car crash injuries I often go upstairs early. When the boys see me taking the wicker basket down from the kitchen beam, they know the evening routine has begun. Several bits and pieces accompany me upstairs, kindly carried by my husband, Neil. My medications, cold drink, grapes and sliced raw carrot in a little pot for their supper. It is the sound of me wielding the small knife to slice the carrot on the stone topped kitchen table that really triggers Operation Bedtime. They appear from wherever. If Cider is upstairs looking out onto the track, his little feet can be heard as he descends the stairs at ever-increasing speed. He hurtles into the kitchen expecting to be given the last slice of carrot — and he usually is. It is then time for bedtime wee wees. Out they go, usually without incident, although I do give a sigh of relief when, upon opening the door, I see the step is dry. Cadfael detests rain. Even a light drizzle causes ears and tail to be clamped down as he very vocally makes his displeasure known. Here again the Jack Russell owners reading this will know what I mean.

I then collect four little sweeties from the Treat Pot and they follow me out of the kitchen, through the study, ready to ascend the stairs. There is a gate fixed with little hinges halfway up. This was erected when Cadfael was a puppy. It gave a barrier so we had some sort of idea where he was. It was then useful with his son Cider and has remained as it is still handy.

Up the first few stairs they go. A quick about-face and they both stand there awaiting the first sweetie. I open the gate, give the treat and they munch happily. Onward up the last few stairs, another about-turn as they await sweetie number two. The treats are actually small tasty dog biscuits. I've called them 'sweeties' for years. I had a pet rabbit called Biscuit — with two Jack Russells, I did not think it wise to keep asking them if they fancied biscuit. They then make their way along the corridor to our bedroom, where I sort things out. I try and clean their teeth every evening. Not as a novelty, but to reduce the build-up of plaque. I know of so many dogs who have had surgery to remove teeth due to plaque build-up or infection. Vets always tell new owners about worming and vaccinations, but some do not seem to encourage teeth cleaning with the same vigour. I do not know why.

In our bedroom, the Whinge language can come to life. Most nights are not interrupted, but sometimes the silence is broken. I am often awake and hearing the first whinge, I lie neath our cosy duvet and wait. An initial whinge could be one of contentedly snuggling down for the night, or an indication something is not right. If there is a second whinge, of louder volume with it starting at a high pitch and going down the scale, then he is thirsty. I know from experience that it is more practical for me to let him out sooner rather than later so he can go and get a drink from the water bowl. He'll then happily return to his pen and sleep through.

I have tried ignoring him but with this particular Jack Russell, that does not work. He'll simply repeat the relevant whinge in ever-increasing volume.

In the morning, a short ascending whinge tells me he is awake and ready to be let out. Without saying anything, I give a wave. He then knows all is well and quietly waits until it is time to get up. Well, most times.

I open Cider's door first and out he bounces. I give him a sweetie. Then his father. He never bounces out, but emerges from under his blanket at a measured pace.

There is logic to the sweetie routine. Cadfael, in particular, can be a fussy eater, but either can have their moment. If they eagerly crunch the treat, I know both are feeling well.

If Cadfael is the master of the language Whinge, then his son Cider has mastered performing arts. At some point between getting up and leaving the bedroom, he will feel the time is right. He then positions himself in a clear space and crouches low. All four legs will be bent. Curtain up and off he goes! Slowly moving across the room, but without gaining height and with a definite look of concentration. As soon as I see this I announce loudly "The morning Po Po IS being performed," in a voice which should command the attention of his father. Cider's little face beams. There is a definite sparkling of the eye and he almost smiles, continuing across the carpet. He is really relishing my attention, even if his father has not even given a cursory glance. I repeat my announcement a couple of times. This makes Cider look very happy. (In case some are wondering why his morning performance is called the Po Po... I will reveal the reason later.)

When all ready, we leave the bedroom and carefully descend the stairs.

I let them out. If it is raining, Cadfael will not be out for long. Getting wet makes him depressed.

Breakfast time! On most days they enjoy it, full tummies, empty bowls and no remaining morsel. If, however, one or both decide that their breakfast offering is not what they would have chosen, stubborn looks appear. I know it is a case of being fussy — bearing in mind the sweetie rule. Bowls are left in position for about ten minutes then removed.

Cadfael can be theatrical. Sometimes he'll stand near his food bowl in a statuesque pose. Hardly a flicker of an eyelid, frozen in time. This scene can last for a while. Then one of two things. Either he will decide to slowly walk towards the bowl and eat his meal, in a manner conveying he is doing me a favour, or the pose continues, before a slow turn and a stiff-legged walk away from the offending meal.

If it is a fussy day for Cider, he will approach, give a glance to see the contents, then carry on past without breaking step.

Right then... breakfast is over.

Both have developed such a finely tuned sense of the impending that they sometimes signal when nothing is there to see. I used to think it was just over enthusiastic Jack Russells, but time after time they have been proved right. Someone is coming. I've calculated this from knowing when people are due and the insistence of the boys that they know what they are barking about. It can sometimes be difficult to shut them up, but I can't have it both ways. They are both such good mobile alarms.

As they have full knowledge if anything is happening on the track, should someone actually stop outside, the boys can't get out fast enough. They race out of the door and usually along to our inner gate by the car park area. If they are already outside, they must make an immediate decision — race to inner gate or to the far end of the cottage and peer through the little gate? If someone is going past, they race to one gate, then hurtle back along the little path to the other. They are very fit! Whichever way they decide to go, it is done at a flat-out charge.

Meeting and greeting visitors is a boisterous affair. Jack Russells are vocal and as Cadfael speaks Whinge, he makes sure he is heard. Cider will do the usual bark but Cadfael does a deep throated monotone whinge. To those who do not know him it could be interpreted as a growl. So to avoid any misunderstanding, I always say, "he is not growling at you, he is speaking." At this point the person usually smiles... possibly with relief... and gives him a friendly pat. As soon as they stand up, Cadfael lets them know that one pat is not sufficient. Whilst 'father' is busy conversing, his son is taking full advantage of the situation. With high pitched squeals of delight, Cider dips his head to be at the right height for biting father's heels. Cider is only small, so he can nip in and out... literally. Cadfael continues his conversation until Cider's gnat-like behaviour finally pushes the boundary of the father-son relationship. He whips round snarling at The Urchin. One does not need to speak Whinge to understand what he is saying! Even so, as everyone tries to manoeuvre along the path to our front door, Cider, in typical Jack Russell style, does not retreat, ducking and diving, still trying to make contact.

Once indoors, normality begins to return. If the postman unfortunately calls at this particular time, then it is back to square one with both racing back to the gate to observe. Both boys are full of vigour and the breed is known for having a strong character. I read in a book, years ago... 'if you are not the obvious choice of Emperor your dog will soon ascend the throne.'

Before relating other tales, let me go back to the beginning of my love for Jack Russells.

I had my first in 1978. I named him 'K9', Dr Who was popular at the time. K9 was of relatively unusual colouring for a Jack. He was all black, apart from a tiny white 'bib' and tan legs and face. He had clean, sharp lines and was an extremely handsome dog.

On one occasion we had a day out at an agricultural show and, when walking around, came to the area where classes for Jack Russells were going to be judged. Most Jacks have a lot more, white on them, with some black and/or brown. There was no realistic chance of mine coming anywhere in the prize line-up due to his colouring. It would take a very strong judge to award K9 anything, always assuming of course, that he was considered to have excellent conformation, movement, teeth etc. In fact, it would be a lost cause before we even entered the ring. However, entries were still being taken. It was a lovely sunny day and carried along with the general hustle and bustle of Jack Russells everywhere, I decided to enter K9. It is always a precarious situation having several Jacks in close proximity. It is a fact that most tend to enjoy a good fight. However, the entry was made and we waited to be called into the show ring. The steward waved his arm, summoning all entrants. A large grassy area had been roped off for the purpose and the sun was shining brightly.

The show ring for Jack Russells is often tucked away at country shows. Quite probably due to no one knowing what physical drama could occur. A seemingly endless line of people entered the ring, each with a Jack Russell. We followed the instructions of the steward, walking in a large circle — dog the side nearest to the judge, who was standing in the middle of the allotted space. The steward indicated that we should cease walking round and form a line down the middle of the ring. Most Jack Russells will have an active walk, mainly due to the fact that they'd quite like to catch the one in front. A line was formed and, if I recall correctly, K9 was third from the end where the judge decided to begin her task.

The judge stood and looked at the first Jack Russell. She studied his conformation and overall appearance, thanked the handler and moved on to the second in line... our neighbour. The same routine, and a thank you, then our turn. She stood and looked, bent down, scooped K9 up in her arms and moved on to entry number four. I felt somewhat bewildered and had no idea what everyone else was thinking. The routine used for dogs one and two was repeated as she moved along the line-up. K9 had shown no resistance to being removed from my side, which in retrospect should have been a relief, as in the years that followed, he became very protective.

All the handlers stood with their dogs next to them, waiting for the judging to be completed. I just stood there, dog-less, trying to look normal.

Obviously, I had been somewhat stunned at her action. Watching as she progressed along the lineup with K9 securely tucked under her arm was certainly not what I had expected. Not sure what to think, the only explanation that made any sense was that K9, due to his unusual Jack Russell colouring, was not considered a suitable dog to show, therefore possibly disqualified.

The final Jack Russell had been judged. She brought K9 back to where I stood alone, and gently placed him back on the ground next to me. She then went and stood in a position from where she could see all the hopeful and expectant contestants. I was not at all hopeful. All hope had drained away the minute K9 had been scooped up and removed from my side. A short wait, as the steward passed her the colourful rosettes. Another quick glance along the line of excited Jack Russells with their expectant handlers and she advanced towards the one she felt superior to all the rest.

I must have said, "Thank you very much," as she handed me the resplendent red rosette and gave a bemused K9 another cuddle. I was in a state of shock so unable to recall much. She did say that he was an outstanding Jack Russell and a very worthy winner. I dread to think what all the other contestants thought.

Quite by chance, I later found out that this judge bred black and tan Jack Russell terriers.

It is down to the many wonderful years K9 and I had together, that I knew Jack Russells were the breed for me. I loved him dearly.

Oscar

He was my second Jack Russell.

I find it upsetting to talk about him. Close friends say it is because we went through such trauma together and that my PTSD is still a factor. They are probably correct. So only a few words.

Oscar was on my lap as I dozed when a passenger in my car, as my husband was driving us home from visiting family, in 2005.

The 100mph impact of the head-on car crash, caused by someone driving on the wrong side of the road, changed our lives forever.

Oscar survived and I became a Blue Badge holder. We had a further three and a half years together with the help of an outstanding veterinary surgeon.

His ashes are in a little terracotta urn which I keep in the bedroom. My son will put them with mine at the relevant time.

My beloved Oscar... how I miss you.

When I felt able to seek another canine companion, I began my search in the usual manner, beginning at my vets. Although there were no relevant adverts on the notice board, I had been using the practice for years and so asked if some of the staff knew of any available Jack Russell puppies. The head nurse let me know of an acquaintance who had mentioned that her Jack Russell bitch recently had a litter. I obtained the telephone number and rang. It was convenient for me to visit, so after returning home to let my husband know of my find, we set off to search for the relevant address.

Having passed through an attractive rural village we soon saw a sign indicating we should turn right down a track. Tracks seem to be quite a relevant factor in my life. Most properties where I have lived have been situated down a track. If I go in search of ducks or other animals it often includes a drive down a track and our present home is along a track. We arrived at the farmhouse where we were warmly greeted and shown into the large country-style kitchen. Four Jack Russell puppies were looking cosy next to their mother. Two dogs and two bitches. I always prefer dogs, so my choice was limited. There was little to choose between them, but I was drawn to one in particular. He was only four days old and so remained with his Jack Russell Mum for a further seven weeks, when we were able to bring him home. I named him 'Cadfael' as in 'Brother'.

He settled in well and a new relationship

began. He was an outstanding looking young dog and, as one vet had confirmed to me, had superb conformation.

Cadfael always had an aristocratic air and a slight aloofness about him. But in established Jack Russell terrier style, he could be a fighter, his wagging tail meaning absolutely nothing if seeing a dog he did not like. Having a particularly unrelenting aversion to Springer Spaniels, he can turn into the Tasmanian Devil in seconds.

His big, brown eyes are like two deep pools, but given the chance, he would soon ascend the Emperor's throne.

I felt sure Cadfael knew Cider was his son straightaway. No dog could have been more forgiving of an errant offspring. Cider's behaviour was similar to that of an annoying gnat. Nipping about in and out of his father's hind legs, striking whenever possible. How Cadfael tolerated him, I have no idea, but he did. Cider still tries to nip Cadfael's back legs when his father is busy greeting people. Every so often, when The Urchin makes contact, his father whips his head round and gives his son a ferocious glare and snarls. Cider takes no notice whatsoever. I often feel the need to assure visitors that they are not trying to kill each other.

Another result of the initial meeting with a lady in the woods — about whom I shall elaborate later – is that she is now my best friend. As I write these words, I am sharing my sofa with Cadfael, Cider, Pig and Po – the puppy my now friend chose to keep.

Remember Cider's morning performances of the Po Po? My friend told me one day that Po had a morning routine. He would crouch low and move slowly across the room, with legs bent. So when Cider began doing the same thing each morning, what else would it be called but the Po Po.

One memory which always brings a smile to my face is when I think back about a sunny day when Cider was two or three years of age. My damaged foot was not as bad as it is now and I'd managed to complete a short walk across grassy fields for charity. After one of my foot operations the rare condition CRPS had developed. A Pain Management Consultant had told me that walking on a suitable surface was the best way to try and keep the pain under control. I had taken Cadfael and Cider, and my friend had Pig and Po plus her tiny Jack Russell cross. There was a small dog show held in a nearby field once the walk was completed. The usual various classes when not a recognised KC show – mixed breeds... just a bit of fun... and so it turned out to be.

We sat in the sun enjoying ice creams as the event got underway. Pig was shown in one of the novelty classes — waggiest tail, I think. She won a rosette. I decided not to enter Cadfael in anything as, although he is a superb dog, I had no doubt that he'd have the entire class in uproar within seconds. Like one of those cards one sees of a fighting ball of terriers when they're meant to be racing and someone asking, "Who's winning?"

My friend pointed out that there was a puppy class and suggested I enter little Cider. I reminded her that he was no longer a puppy — she'd apparently overlooked this minor point. Getting carried away with the idea, she tried to encourage me. "Enter him, enter him... he'll come last, but he'll have fun" she enthused. Seeing my reluctance to make a spectacle of myself and me in turn seeing her disappointment at my preventing Cider from having fun... I made the throwaway remark, "You can take him in if you like." Before I had time to clarify that I was only joking, she had gone. However, she soon reappeared with the joyful words, "He's entered." Entered he may have been, but I was not going to be the person on the other end of the lead. The class was called. I remained seated and was minder of the four nonparticipants, whilst Cider was whisked away to make his show debut... in the puppy class! The judging did not take long no questions were asked. To my utter amazement and surprise, Cider, aka The Urchin, did not come last and he did have fun.

With his tail wagging happily and wearing a look of pride he left the ring with a brightly coloured rosette attached to his collar. It now hangs alongside his picture in our study. How? Why? These questions will never be answered, but a jolly good day was had by all... especially Cider and my friend.

Some years ago, I had said to my husband that as Cadfael was such an outstanding Jack Russell, I felt sure there was a good chance that someone would want to use him as a stud dog (for breeding). I finished the conversation by saying that if this did happen and a litter of puppies was born, I would want to keep one.

A couple of years after that, on a Saturday as I recall, my husband was at home and friends were staying for the weekend. I was walking Cadfael with one of them, having entered the woods at the end of our track. Nearing the building by the main entrance to the Country Park, I was pointing out the wood carving of an owl on the archway. A lady, without a dog, came up to me. She apologised for interrupting our walk and said she knew that what she was going to ask could sound odd. "Your dog is superb, I'd really like to use him as a stud dog for my Jack Russell bitch." I was not that surprised, seeing as I'd prophesised this occurrence, some time before. We began to chat about the possibility. I said that whilst I was not to averse to this, I would have to see the bitch to approve the breeding. My friend and I listened to the description of her Jack Russell and everything sounded fine. I felt the slightly quirky name of her bitch — 'Pig' — could indicate that she and I could get on well. I like quirky and naming a Jack Russell bitch 'Pig', is definitely quirky. Of slight concern was the fact that Pig was already in season, so not much time for lengthy consideration. I said if she could bring Pig along to our cottage the next day, Sunday and if I felt all was well, then things could proceed. I would not charge a stud fee, but would like pick of the litter. This was agreed. I explained where I lived and my friend and I returned home through the woods.

My husband was relaxing in the sitting room. "You know the conversation we had a year or so ago about someone probably wanting to use Cadfael as a stud dog and me keeping a puppy from a litter... well, the bitch is coming here tomorrow,"... and so she did. Pig was a nice bouncy little Jack Russell, smooth coated like Cadfael and with good conformation.

The outcome of this little episode was that in December that year, I received a phone call from Pig's owner letting me know that the puppies were on the way. We had kept in touch throughout and there was a happy and exciting outcome with a litter of six healthy puppies. I visited when they were a few days old… oh, they were all so adorable… and several times more, before choosing the one I wanted. I usually prefer dogs to bitches and so had a choice from four. The one most similar in colour to his father, mainly brown and white with touches of black, was the smallest.

Luckily, we only lived a few miles apart and so there were several visits before he was old enough to come home. Cadfael can be a fighter and, whilst most dogs will not go for a puppy, I could not take any chances. With this in mind, I felt it would be best to take Cadfael with me when we went to collect his son. Knowing what Jacks can be like, I did not think it sensible to return home, open the front door and for Cadfael to see what he could consider to be an intruder coming on his territory, albeit only eight weeks of age. I even purchased a muzzle, just in case things did not go smoothly. However, things could not have gone any better. Not the slightest sign of aggression.

We returned home with father and son Jack Russells. I decided to name puppy, 'Cider' as Cadfael's mother was called 'Scrumpy', which is a rough, strong cider often made on farms. Cider, otherwise known as 'The Urchin', quickly settled into life at our cottage, causing havoc as puppies do.

In good weather, Cadfael and Cider and I often enjoy an energetic play outside. When I call out, "Fun and Games," both come running into the kitchen. Cadfael always has his turn first. Since purchasing a large inflated ball when on holiday in Wales a few years ago, this is the toy of their choice for the physical exercise which is about to happen. It is quite amazing the level of noise two Jack Russells can achieve when they know their favourite game is about to commence. I can only open the front door a minimal distance due to Cider trying to join us, but Cadfael and I manage to squeeze ourselves through. The Urchin (Cider) knows he has to wait for his father to have first turn, but still barks excitedly trying to get outside at the same time as us.

Cadfael and I manage to exit onto the front step. Cadfael, keeping his eyes on the ball I hold aloft, manoeuvres himself down the three pergola steps onto the lawn more or less on hind leg tippy toes, barking excitedly. Once there, he is keen for fun and games to begin. The ball is attached to a plastic spiral cord and Cadfael's preferred style of game is for me to swing the ball in a large circle. Cadfael races around desperately trying to make contact. It is a large ball, about twice the size of a football. Every now and then, with an extra energetic lunge, he does manage to clench his teeth around where the spiral cord is attached to the ball. As I shout, "Give," I manage to make him let go and the game resumes. He races along as the ball circles, until after several minutes of supreme effort, ducking and diving, I think it time to cease the exercise. I say, "Bring it in, bring it in," and Cadfael closely follows the ball for our return inside. Once back in the kitchen, his reward is a piece of cheese. The Urchin is still keen for his turn, but has sufficient time and interest to lunge in and try and take some of his father's reward. He does not succeed.

Cider's turn. Out we go, managing to prevent his still keen father from joining us and the noise from both can be heard as we reach the lawn. Cider prefers leaping up and down instead of running round in circles. He is much smaller than his father but often manages to catch me out by attaining a height which I feel would be far out of his reach… well over a metre off the ground. With his ability to surprise me, he sometimes does manage to catch the spiral cord. The command 'give' works well and he lets go… most times. As he flies through the air with all the balance and expertise of a trapeze artist, I find myself talking him through the twists and turns like one would coach a gymnast. "Flight and height, flight and height. Very good. Bit more height. Oh well done." Then the grand finale. He crouches low in readiness, his eyes fixed on the ball as it swirls past. "NOW!" I shout when I think the time is right. He springs up, his little body stretched out as he gains height. Our sloping lawn gives him the chance to fly and for a few seconds his little head is near mine as he soars past. A passing thought comes into my mind… Cider's ability is quite amazing… and I fantasize about him achieving fame on 'Britain's Got Talent?' "Oh well done, well done, excellent work," I say, as the game concludes. "Bring it in, bring it in". An exhilarated little Jack follows me indoors and devours his piece of cheese with great relish.

When the weather permits, inasmuch as it is cool, the boys accompany me in the car when I go out. Since the crash on that fateful day in 2005 I take no chances. My dogs each travel in separate pens secured by chains to fixings in the back of the car. Proper mountaineering clips (carabiners) hold them in place. On some occasions when my husband and I are both travelling, they wear specially designed car harnesses, again clipped onto the seat belt by carabiners. A pillow and blanket on the lap of the passenger enables them to snuggle down with the opportunity to look through the window.

Most times I prefer to drive myself, but when on the way to one of my hospital appointments my husband sometime takes the wheel, I find it very calming having the boys on my lap as I run my fingers across their soft fur.

When sharing a life with dogs, one is never alone. I can tell them anything. They always listen and never question. They just give love. Having two Jack Russells can be a full-on experience and one I treasure daily. I cannot envisage a day when I do not have a Jack Russell terrier.

The Little Gate

This simple little gate has apparently been at our sixteenth century cottage for generations; untreated and unpainted. Over twenty-five years ago, some elderly strangers called by. They had lived here as children and were pleased to see the little gate still here — proving it's not always necessary to get out a paintbrush.

1991 was the year it became necessary for us to seek a rurally situated property where we could envisage spending our future.

A year or so earlier, we had bought a new build near Bedford. A complete change from our usual type of property and area. Thinking back, it was such a wrong decision, but at the time, health scares, together with a feeling that maybe we would enjoy a more socially active life near a town, clouded judgement.

It did not take long to realise our mistake.

So we began a search for a suitable home in the county of Herefordshire. That area has wonderful countryside, pretty villages and everything needed for a return to rural life. Being close to the England-Wales border was also a relevant factor.

My husband is Welsh and we had met many years previously in the car park of an inn just over the border into Wales, when I was on holiday. He was born in a small stone cottage where his family lived. It was approached by walking up a cwm leading through some woods... just off the Hereford road to Brecon. Water was drawn from a well and light provided by paraffin or candles. All can sound quaint and appealing, but in reality, life would have been very hard.

We have since visited his former home and it looked a really interesting cottage of character, but I can imagine the hardship of life there, caring for a large family with no inside water supply and without electricity. The appearance of the property had changed somewhat, as over the years, owners had brought it up to standard for modern day living. It is said never go back, but in this instance my husband was interested to see how his first family home had changed. I was keen to see in reality the property I had, for years, pictured in my mind.

A friend who lived in the county told me of a cottage for sale which she passed when walking her dogs... I will elaborate on this later. It was situated on a track which she accessed from fields leading down from a local manor house. A short time later, my husband and I travelled to view the property, which we learned had not been lived in for over four years. The written particulars were sparse... a 16th century stone cottage, two up, two down, no services and with land extending to just under five acres. The agents given the task of selling the property were based miles away. Our contact with them had resulted in a key being posted to us for viewing when convenient. Access was not easy, it certainly did not look as though anyone had battled through the brambles and briars for a very long time. Ivy covered the walls like a large oversized coat of green. We managed to pick our way through the undergrowth without mishap and made our way around the back, as we searched for an entrance. It turned out that there was only one door in and out of this place of history and rather unusually, the front door was around the back. Decades later, I still think it sounds a little odd when I tell prospective visitors that the front door is around the back.

The old, rusty key resembled a smaller version of the type one sees in films and books for opening the huge doors of fairy tale castles. My husband inserted it into the large keyhole. There were a few creaks and with a little pushing the old wooden door slowly opened. A couple of steps inside onto flagstones and we were taken back in time. An old, blackened well-used kitchen range was on the left in an inglenook. A large, sturdy crane was above it, securely fixed onto the left-hand wall, so it could be swung back and forth when a pan or kettle was to be suspended over the fire. A bread oven in the wall on the right of the range, completed the old kitchen scene. Wonderful. There was a room on the right from where the stairs rose and one room with a dirt floor running the full length of the cottage along the back... or front... depending how one decided which was the front and which was the back! That would have been where the animals would have been housed during the winter months. That part had a catslide roof. A catslide roof is a pitched roof where one side stretches further down than the other.

It did not take either of us long to know that this basic little stone building, virtually uninhabitable as it was, had the potential to be the rural retreat for which we searched. Negotiations and communication were done by phone or letter and on 1st August 1991 the little cottage was ours. Having been empty for so long the kitchen felt cold and the rooms without purpose. The whole place felt as though it had been abandoned due to some unforeseen reason. Left to stand alone, unwanted and unloved.

Making ourselves known to the neighbours, a couple of fields away, gave us an insight into how this little cottage had been home to a single lady all her life. Indeed, it had been both home and a place of work for generations of her family. For many years she had lived in it alone. Our neighbours who have become such good friends, told us all they knew and as we learned more, the place took on a whole new perspective. The lady, who we think was named Evelyn, apparently had her daytime cats and her nighttime cats. Too many to be inside at the same time, so she organised a rota. She had also kept goats which would have been her source of fresh milk. There had been an outside privy, long since succumbed to the ravages of time. Over the years it has been noticeable that all plants flourish in the area where that little private shed had once stood and the rhubarb we planted, always does exceedingly well.

A couple of original meat hooks hung from the kitchen ceiling. To preserve this particular feature, the kitchen ceiling has not been altered and it is a permanent reminder of times past. I should point out that my husband, due to his high standard of workmanship, would have much preferred to repair the rather shabby ceiling, but I felt that would have removed an important feature, so in the true spirit of renovation to retain character, it remained as was.

Large ceiling beams were in the rooms and they were all painted a pale green. On the outside the windows had bricks placed over them to give a curved decoration feature. They were all painted green. Two large thin wooden barrels were found outside… they were green. An old metal container had flakes of green paint clinging to it and several other remnants of times past, not to break the theme, were also green.

The process of sand blasting was considered as a method of removing the paint from the beams, but only for a short while. My allergies and the thought of all the dust and mess, caused us to dismiss the idea almost as soon as we had thought of it.

Something very interesting and never before seen, was a barn, about 30ft x 10ft. Nothing surprising about that, apart from it being totally made from tins. 'Baked Bean' type tins, with top and base removed, slit up one side and flattened into rectangles. Dozens and dozens were then nailed on to a simple wooden frame to construct the barn. It had then been painted with black tar and it stood in sombre splendour. Quite possibly unique. Even knowing this, we could not let this masterpiece remain and so it was demolished with due reverence shown for the many man-hours it would have taken to construct years before.

It was important to have the services connected as soon as possible... electricity and water. There were several natural springs on the land and so a company specialising in drilling boreholes for water came along and began the process. Due to the number of springs it was generally thought they would strike oil... or in this case, water. Two days later and they left, having been unable to tap into a suitable source. Very disappointing. So, like the majority of people, we are now on mains water supply. A septic tank which resembled a bright yellow submarine was duly delivered and with some manhandling, was dropped into the large hole dug by my husband.

Here, I sing the praises of my husband who has done the entire renovation work himself, apart from the very occasional help from one of his brothers.

Obviously, some decisions were made taking into account his knowledge as a carpenter and builder, but on the whole the division of labour worked well. He doing the work and me having the design and decoration ideas and sourcing the various paints etc. in keeping with a period property.

The two existing bedrooms have vaulted ceilings with beams. One room required a new substantial beam… a purlin. We sourced one and it was duly delivered. So, one purlin outside on the track needing to be hoisted up and manoeuvred into the room via an upstairs window and fixed into position to support the ceiling. Not so much as one man and his dog, but one man and his purlin. It was about 12ft in length and extremely heavy, being a solid piece of oak. The day dawned when the purlin was to be lifted from the ground outside and fixed into position inside. One of his brothers came to help with this daunting task.

Thinking back, it was an incredible accomplishment as between them, with various ropes and sheer strength, the purlin was lifted from the ground and slowly pulled up the side of the cottage. It swayed slightly as it rose inch by inch until level with an upstairs window opening. It was then carefully steadied from swinging round and guided through the window and manhandled into the bedroom, where with the use of various blocks and platforms it was raised up and fitted in place to secure the ceiling. A remarkable feat of strength.

Gradually the little cottage grew as we were able to extend it lengthwise to include a sitting room with a master bedroom above. All the work to renovate has been done sympathetically and in keeping with the style of the property. The renovations would have been completed years ago had the car crash not happened in 2005. Since then I have had several operations and after each, my husband has taken over the day-to-day care of me and the animals, thus delaying the renovation work.

As some of you may be aware, it is often necessary to take a medication to avoid deep vein thrombosis after surgery. Whilst I have no problem with injecting animals and would not be averse to injecting people, there is no way I could inject myself. Returning home after one operation, I had been given the medication to take in tablet form. I have many allergies and they were making me unwell. When chatting to a visiting friend she happened to mention her ability to give injections. "Excellent," said I, "Can you fit me into your daily schedule and inject my stomach daily for a while, please." She readily agreed and for the next week or so, she'd pop in and do the necessary. I will always be grateful to her for doing this for me. She had the perfect knack and it was a painless procedure. Better than many I have had done in hospitals.

After a while, the renovation work was mainly done at weekends and in the evenings, with my husband going to work during the day. Whilst it has taken a lot longer than initially envisaged, at no time have we regretted the decision made over two decades ago, to purchase our little piece of Herefordshire.

Previous to our arrival here in 1991, the land had only been grazed by goats for generations and having been goat free for several years, the land was ready for new livestock. I had a flock of pedigree rare breed sheep and the land was quite suitable for them. They did well here and after years of breeding and showing, when I decided to sell them, someone bought the flock sight unseen, knowing the established quality.

As the full renovation was always going to be a long-term project, albeit extended through no fault of our own, it was not going to be at the exclusion of all else. As time passed, we began visiting North Wales for holidays and my husband resumed playing golf. Having this normality included in our lives kept things in perspective and enabled us to keep our dream alive.

As explained earlier, a good friend had discovered this cottage when walking her dogs from the home in which she lived. Her home was situated in the grounds of a large country manor estate, which had many acres of land.

I had visited the period farmhouse where she and her family lived many times and we had become good friends. Over thirty years on and we still are. The type of friendship where, even if we have not met up for a number of years, when we do, the conversation carries on as if we last met the day before.

She would follow a path taking her and dogs along the edges of corn fields, until coming down to a track, when by turning right she could more or less do a circuit via a farmyard and head back home. If turning left, she could walk along an ancient cart track until reaching a lane, turn right to head up a tiny lane and head home through woodland paths. She was aware that my husband and I were searching for a cottage and had noticed a small sign amongst some trees on the left of the track. It was only just visible and after peering through the leafy twigs and branches, she read the magic words — For Sale. She wasted no time in telling me about her find and thus the process had begun.

My husband lost no time in making living conditions suitable for us. We would sit in the old kitchen aka HQ, designing the layout and making plans for how our currently damp little cottage would gradually become the cottage of our dreams.

Before major constructional work could begin, we had to clear access along the track and make a proper entrance. Some old trees had to be cut down to open up the place to daylight and make it safe from falling branches. That in itself was a lot of hard work. Doing it all by ourselves meant everything was hard work and it all took a great deal of time. It was not surprising the place had remained unsold for so long. It reminded me of a small version of the ruined home of Miss Havisham. Hardly visible through overgrown trees, brambles and hedges, it had gradually become hidden from time.

Upon entering the property, the sense of history and times past were immediately felt. One could imagine the horse and cart coming along the track after taking provisions to local areas. The stories the old horseshoes could tell. The meat hooks in the kitchen ceiling. The old range with simmering pots over, the bread oven where many a loaf would have been baked. One could 'see' Evelyn, the last person to live here before us, seated in front of the range, warming herself from the heat of the burning coals. Going through to stabled animals in the back, flickering candles lighting her way. Then up the creaking stairs to bed.

But now it was our time, months turned to years and it was encouraging to see the transformation gradually taking place. We were very pleased at the way in which our chosen design plan was working. Three bedrooms and three reception rooms, lots of lovely oak beams throughout and the interior decor, which was basically my responsibility had all come together so well.

I recall one sunny day, a few years ago, it was early in the afternoon and there was a knock at the door… remember the front door is around the back. I opened the large solid oak door made by my husband. Several people were standing there. They asked if I was the owner and when informed that my husband and I were indeed the owners, began to tell their tale. They were related to Evelyn and had lived here many years ago. Tales of life here as it had been. Remember the large green wooden barrels? As children it was their task to pluck the chicken or goose destined for dinner and put the feathers in one of the barrels. When the barrel was full, it meant there were sufficient feathers for an eiderdown. Another family member would undertake the task of making it. Such a personal little gem of history. I think it had been a happy home from the way they spoke of their time here, even the regular trudge to the outside privy. They smiled as I told how anything planted in that area flourished.

They were all so pleased to hear how we valued the history of the place and were trying to renovate it sympathetically and felt how it had once been a happy home.

The highlight of the visit from their point of view, was what they had seen as their feet once again trod the track, as they approached the cottage once called home. "The little gate is still here," they all enthused happily. They remembered the few planks of wood, nailed together in simple style generations ago, to make a little entrance gate. Indeed, it was still here and still is. No brush of paint nor preservative to protect it, yet it remains upright. It is no longer used, but remains a symbol of times past. A time portal to generations past.

Reigning Cockerels

My new young cockerel — he looks splendiferous. Came upon this word by chance, as I did him. He made his presence known within minutes of arrival. Totally splendiferous.

We have been very fortunate in having the same lovely neighbours for twenty-seven years and we have become such good friends. A year or so ago, they felt the time had come to leave our little patch of rural tranquillity and move to the edge of town. They had kept a wide selection of poultry during this time — chickens of various breeds, shapes and colours, ducks in a similar way and a goose called Bobby. He would wander the paddocks with his feathered friends, quite happy to be the only goose. A few years ago, Bobby laid an egg and became Bobbie. Dogs, rabbits and a cat completed their animal family. It was not going to be possible to take any poultry with them, so they set about finding new homes for them all.

I popped round one Friday morning to see how the process was going. They looked pleased when telling me all had been found new homes. All, that is apart from One Eyed Cecil, a Pekin bantam cockerel aged about ten years. It sounded as if there was only one place Cecil would be going... and it wouldn't be to the house on the edge of town. It is often impossible to rehome any cockerel, let alone an elderly one. I thought about it all night and next morning saw me once more sitting in our neighbours' kitchen. I said that if One Eyed Cecil can think and live like a duck, then he could come to ours and live with my ducks. That settled, I retraced my steps back up the lane and along the track to our cottage.

A couple of days later and our neighbour appeared, carrying a cardboard box. One Eyed Cecil had arrived! He was quite a bit larger than I had expected. All the banties I had known had been quite dinky with clean cut lines. Cecil was without doubt, what I would call a large 'fluffball'. A soft smokey grey in colour with puffed up fluffy feathers. He was a gentle bird… easy to catch and pick up. He quickly adapted to life with my ducks and after two days was always the first one into Duck House 1, at bedtime, choosing a corner where he could snuggle into the straw and go to sleep. One Eyed Cecil was perfectly happy living with my ducks.

A week passed and when next in their kitchen, I commented that they must both feel very relieved at having rehomed all the birds. "Oh yes," was the reply, "it only leaves Billy the Kid."

"Who — what?" said I.

It was explained that Billy the Kid was an elderly cockerel who had been hatched from one of their eggs about ten years previously.

I had heard both One Eyed Cecil and Billy the Kid crowing back and forth for years. Our properties were separated by a couple of fields and I had enjoyed hearing the 'conversations' between the cockerels. Such a natural country sound.

I was aware of a sense of anticipation as I sat

at their kitchen table drinking the steaming hot chocolate from a mug decorated with a rural scene. At this point I noticed that the mug showed a resplendent cockerel strutting across a farmyard. I felt sure my drink was in this particular mug just by chance... well, fairly sure.

Then — "We wondered if Billy the Kid could live in your car park area and barn?... ...he was hatched here from one of our eggs... he is elderly and would be very content with a daily handful of corn."

It did not take me long. "When will you bring him round?" I asked.

During the many years of friendship, both of our neighbours had come round to our place numerous times to let out dogs, feed cats and rabbits when we were away or I was in hospital for further surgery due to my car crash injuries.

Billy the Kid would take up residence in our 'car park' and the barn which is in the same area. In case any reader thinks he would spend his days pacing up and down on tarmac, I will explain.

Our cottage is approached via a very rough track which leads off a lane, behind a wood. Entry onto the property is through a twelve foot wooden gate. Once through that, there is a large open area... our car park. A very old barn is on the left and an ancient red brick building on the right. There are several trees on the approach to the old orchard as one passes the barn and our wood store would give him lots of interest.

A few days later Billy the Kid arrived. He seemed quite content to have been carried up the lane and along the track. In through the gate came neighbour and Billy. Whilst we chatted about the impending move, Billy gazed around the patch which would be his home. Once on the ground he pottered about, gradually exploring the area. He is a large cockerel and as very elderly in poultry years, walks slowly, moving his legs in a slightly circular manner. He has a pleasant nature and quickly settled into my routine. Whereas Cecil slept with my ducks, Billy slept in the barn. Plenty of straw bales and wood piles made it quite enticing and the pièce de résistance was an old tea chest. Turned on its side and filled with straw it made a lovely, cosy bed.

Both cockerels had continued to converse, even when One Eyed Cecil was with my ducks and Billy the Kid still next door. But now they could have more serious discussions and when Cecil decided it was a day to fly over the fence and prowl around our garden, there was only a metal gate separating them. Cockerels are well known for aggressive fighting, sometimes with devastating results. Although these two had lived in separate paddocks previously, they knew about each other and apart from a few raised hackles on occasions as they peered eye-to-eye through the gate, both were content living here.

Nearly two years on and we have new neighbours.

Our good friends have happily settled into their new home — a bright modern bungalow, close to the town and with all facilities nearby. Indeed, it was the right time for them to go. They still have their dogs, rabbits and a cat and the lovely garden is of a manageable size with plenty of space for growing vegetables. No longer the work of looking after poultry with all that involves and no longer having to keep the paddocks maintained. Life is now more leisurely. We are still the very best of friends and whilst it is no longer a case of walking along the track and lane to visit, we meet regularly for the usual natter across the kitchen table or shopping expeditions, as we are only a few miles apart.

Every morning, I let out my ducks, decide which little group is going where and trundle the relevant ones out to the orchard in the little trolley constructed by my husband. Breakfast is then given and whilst the quacks tuck in, I let Billy the Kid out of the barn, feed him then return to the duck house area to feed One Eyed Cecil. Some days he spends in a secure area in the orchard. Others, he potters around the garden and says hello to Billy the Kid through the gate.

One morning a few weeks ago, when the ducks exited from Duck House 1 in their usual excited manner, Cecil was not with them. I lifted the roof in the usual way and looked inside. He was sitting in his chosen corner, but showed no interest in coming out.

I picked him up... he showed no sign of stress nor pain. I gently put him back to rest whilst I went to check the ducks. Cecil could decide whether or not to leave the duck house. I was surprised to hear a cockerel crow coming from the duck area. I retraced my steps and there he was... One Eyed Cecil standing on the side of the duck house, proudly lifting his head high and crowing loudly. I watched for a few minutes then placed him back on the straw, putting a dish of his favourite food and drinking water nearby. By early evening, I could see he had not moved much, but still no sign of distress. I felt that he would soon be leaving us. Rather than there be the risk of the ducks inadvertently walking on him, I picked him up once more and made him comfortable for the night in a separate carrier. I wished him well.

Early next morning I went to check. He had passed away during the night. It had been a gentle, peaceful death. If only we could all have such a calm passing. I believe him crowing proudly the previous morning was him saying goodbye to us all.

I always feel sad when one of my pets die and so wrote a small piece about him, posting it on the sites of the Poultry Clubs to which I belong.

R I P One Eyed Cecil.

My photo and words about One Eyed Cecil on social media were well received. Many wrote of their understanding about my loss.

One member posted a photo of a very colourful cockerel, seemingly about to enjoy a snack. She wrote of her desperate search to find a new home for him and asked if I could take him in view of my recent loss.

I replied not at this time but went on to explain that I would need another at some point.

Soon after the arrival of Billy the Kid, it became apparent that he was lonely. Whilst living next door, he had other chickens for company. Here he did not and that needed to change. I wrote posts for my Poultry Clubs explaining the situation and asked if anyone was trying to rehome a chicken, preferably one no longer laying eggs. I much prefer duck eggs and having a laying hen would be an unwanted complication. One member posted a photo and some details of a chicken she could no longer keep. Most poultry keepers want their birds to lay eggs and this particular hen did not. Could this be the required friend for Billy the Kid?

A few messages were exchanged and a time

and date arranged for us to meet, so that I could collect and return home with 'Rhoda'.

It is always slightly disconcerting meeting a stranger for this kind of thing. One sits in the car, intently watching the faces of everyone driving into the car park, waiting expectantly for a box to appear containing the precious cargo. After about twenty minutes I gave up and decided to go and explore the inside of the Discovery Centre. I'd only just gone through the door when a lady came in clutching a box. Rhoda had arrived! The lady and I exchanged pleasantries and having talked chickens for a while, went outside to my car. I'd brought along a good-sized carrier and Rhoda's then Mum transferred her. Our journey back was uneventful.

Upon arrival I decided to leave Rhoda in the large carrier which I put outside in our car park, putting food and water in with her. Billy the Kid had immediately shown interest upon her arrival and had moved up to the carrier with as much dexterity as he could muster. He spent the rest of the day standing like a sentry on guard whilst Rhoda dozed and snacked at her leisure. Late afternoon I proceeded to the barn bearing the carrier in which Rhoda sat. Billy the Kid followed along. Upon entering, I closed the doors... just in case. Her previous owner had explained in our exchange of messages, that Rhoda really loved uncooked porridge oats as a treat. Consequently, porridge oats had been purchased. Set out for their first tea together were portions of corn and the oats. The carrier was opened… Billy waited expectantly whilst Rhoda stepped through the door with only a sideways glance at him, as she advanced towards the awaiting oats with the kind of strut usually only seen by models on the catwalk. Billy knew his place and thus it remained.

During the next couple of days, I gave a lot of thought to the request I'd received from the poultry club member asking if I wanted another cockerel to replace Cecil. As I put previously, it is often a worry and can be a problem trying to find a home for male birds. Approaching winter is the most difficult time and for people unable to find a suitable home there is usually only one way to go. It can sometimes be better to despatch the bird humanely rather than take it to a unknown fate at a poultry auction.

I would need another one in the not too distant future, as Billy the Kid was very elderly in poultry years. The crowing of a cockerel is such a basic country sound and one I have enjoyed for years, I would always want to have one if possible. If me having the cockerel would solve her problem and prevent him from having to be despatched then I would offer him a home now. The fact that her boy looked so colourful in the photo, was one of the reasons he had remained in my thoughts.

I contacted her letting her know that he could have a home here.

Thus, it was agreed, that she would bring him to ours on a Sunday morning... the day after we returned from holiday.

As it turned out, we were very lucky to make it back home on Saturday. Very heavy and unrelenting rain had caused serious flooding. We were diverted off the A5 before reaching the A49 roundabout. Things went from bad to worse as nearly all the minor roads were flooded. Abandoned cars showed the serious risk of us not making it home. The occasional splutter from the Yeti engine did not inspire confidence, but after many worrying miles we made it. Our housesitter had let me know that the normal way in to the village was flooded and the lane under the railway bridge was impassable. But by mid-afternoon we were home, via the woods.

Sunday morning, I did the ducks and fed Rhoda and Billy. I was keen to see my new cockerel who had looked so eye-catching in the photo. He looked slightly boat-shaped as he was bending forward to pick up a snack so I was keen to see him in the feathers, so to speak. It was the fact that he looked such a vision of colour in the photo, which had caused me to reconsider having another cockerel at this time, plus his future, or lack of, if I did not. My plan was to let him live wth my ducks in the same way as Cecil.

A car pulled up outside and it was indeed the lady with 'my' cockerel. I had wanted a name for him that would reflect his wonderful colouring — oranges, golds, flame. Several possibilities had come to mind but nothing was quite right. A poultry-keeping friend lives nearby. She has accompanied me on several expeditions to the back of beyond in the quest for ducklings or eggs to hatch. A few days earlier I had forwarded the photo of the cockerel to her hoping she may suggest the ideal name. She did. 'Russet'…perfect.

So Russet had made the journey in a cardboard box on the back seat of the car. He was carefully removed and carried along the path and into the duck area as I led the way.

His breeder owner had told me that he'd hatched at Easter from a blue egg. His father was a Cheshire Blue — mostly white with some dark spots and his mother a bantam. In view of Russet's flamboyant colouring, the bantie must indeed have been an extremely colourful bird. Russet looked magnificent.

The best time to introduce a new bird to others is at bedtime. Popping it into a poultry house as dusk falls usually avoids quarrels. They all go to sleep and come out next morning as friends. However, it was only 11 o'clock in the morning and we had to do something with Russet.

There was nothing else to do except put him down somewhere. No point in dithering about, so he was gently placed on the large board which covers the duck feed station. He stood there for all of three seconds, then with a flourish of his wings, rose up into the air like a phoenix and landed on the top of one of the two poles between which trellis is stretched, where my husband used to grow the runner beans. Not a major problem in itself but he was quite close to the duck boundary fence, the other side of which is one of our fields, currently overgrown with weeds and at a lower level. No possibility at all of me getting in there to find him if he decided to fly over. My foot injury is severe and so limits where I can go and what I can do.

We stood looking at him, whilst he looked at us. There was nothing to do but leave him to it. I put some corn on the feed station and we left. The previous owner was very happy for him to have a new home with me and I was pleased to have such a beautiful cockerel.

A short time later Russet descended from the pole back onto the board. As I watched him, he decided to fly over the other fence and landed on the lawn.

This was all rather worrying, especially as the parting comments from the breeder was that he often liked to roost in a tree. Apparently, she'd use a suitable item to carefully dislodge him from his chosen branch, shine a light into his face as he landed — as chickens can't see in the dark, pick him up and put him to bed. Mmmmm!

Whilst Russet walked around the garden, I went over to our car park to ponder the situation. Rhoda and Billy the Kid were doing nothing to indicate that they were aware of the new arrival. I thought about it logically. Russet would be more likely to settle if he had a hen for company. I could move Billy in with the ducks, Moby and Co., and Russet could go into the car park area where Rhoda would act as his anchor. Billy was well used to my ducks, as they often potter around the area where he and Rhoda live. I decided to think about it for an hour or so whilst I and Ratty cat went to visit an elderly friend who lived nearby. Whilst there I decided the surest way for Russet to be secure was for him and Billy to swap living areas. I rang my husband to ask if he would try and perform this task. "No chance," was his reply. I would therefore undertake the task myself when I returned early afternoon.

As I pulled up in front of our gate an hour or so later, I was somewhat alarmed to see Russet in the car park. My husband told me that he had been able to make the swap, having firstly encased his hands in the heavy-duty gauntlets usually reserved for annual manoeuvres with the Christmas tree. All tickety-boo then… and so it was until bedtime.

At dusk we both looked around the car park, as I'd asked for help to usher Rhoda and Russet into the barn for the first night at his new home.

I talk to everyone here and my chickens are no exception. Not just the "Good morning, breakfast." But a more in-depth chat. Asking if they had a good night, a brief weather report, what I am serving for breakfast, etc. You may think I am in need of help at this point, but my years with animals has proved without doubt that the more you put in with animals, the more you get out. I talk to them… they talk to me, to the best of their ability. It is great. So, calling "Rhoda, bedtime" the search began.

We found Rhoda hovering around our large entrance gate. Russet was nowhere to be seen.

I peered under shrubs, behind stone slabs and pots, with a passing question, "Where is he, Rhoda?" She did her usual mutter and chatter and remained where she was. She did not look a happy chicken. Remember the rule that a cockerel will not abandon a hen. How wrong is that!

I opened the gate and walked through. Looked left on the grassed area towards the lane… nothing. Looked the other way and there he was. Walking away down the track at a gentle pace and for all I knew, leaving us forever. There was no way either of us would be able to go past to turn him. The only option was to back off and hope he'd retrace his steps… and almost immediately he did. Once back on home ground, it was not difficult to usher Rhoda and Russet into the barn for the night and serve them their belated tea, closing the door securely as we left.

Monday morning, I was up early to let them out. But not as early as Russet. There he was, wandering around the car park welcoming in the day, crowing with gusto.

Having a cockerel can make the use of an electronic alarm wholly redundant. Cockerels crow mainly first thing in the morning. Their in-built body clock works on a 23.8 hour cycle and a recent study shows that they do not need light to know of approaching dawn. Some will crow at any time — and there are several reasons for this — making himself known to other cockerels, a warning and sometimes just for conversation. The sound of a crowing cockerel is one of the most recognisable sounds on the planet and to me, one of the best.

So, Russet was out and about… Rhoda was not. I opened the barn doors and there she stood, looking somewhat perplexed, having been abandoned by Russet so early in their relationship. I set out their breakfast and went to feed Billy and the ducks.

Billy the Kid had settled into life with them without a problem. He was with friends and had plenty of room in which to potter.

Monday late afternoon, I passed both Rhoda and Russet on my way to the barn.

As I prepared their tea, I spoke to them loud enough so they could hear, incorporating Russet's name as I went through the menu. I deliberately made it obvious that their food was about to be served. The sound of corn being poured into a dish and making Rhoda aware that her favourite oats were on the menu had the desired result. Both entered the barn and tucked in to their meal. Barn doors shut, I retraced my steps with a feeling of relief. That was short-lived. Before I reached our cottage door, I could hear crowing coming from the car park… and yes, he was out again. The only way he could be doing this was by flying up and squeezing through between the gaps in the top horizontal planks. I returned, shooed him back in and left.

Tuesday morning was initially a replay of Monday. There he was looking cocky as he threw back his head and crowed… mmm, I felt sure the word 'cocky' was derived from the word cockerel. I was determined to put an end to Russet doing as he pleased. He probably exited the barn in the early hours, but I could not take the risk as he may have been out all night and there is always the possibility of foxes.

That Tuesday I was due to take Ratty (Ratatouille) the cat to visit residents living in a nearby care home. He usually goes once a week and is much loved by all.

The clocks had 'gone back' in the early hours of the previous Sunday morning, so it was getting dark earlier. I'd let Neil know I would try and return home before light failed as Russet was not yet used to the routine and from what the breeder had said, it was a distinct possibility that he would roost in a tree if left to his own devices.

It was still daylight when Ratty and I visited our last resident for that day. Ratty sprawled across her lap purring contentedly. When I next looked outside... oh dear... it was quite dark. We said our goodbyes and returned home.

I arrived back, let Ratty out and went to check in the barn. Rhoda was snuggled down on some straw. No sign of Russet. I had very much hoped he would have gone in with Rhoda. I searched all the nooks and crannies in the car park area... around the log piles, the heap of stones to be used on our cottage, generally everywhere. I only had a small torch and the beam was not sufficiently bright to shine right up into the trees to see if Russet had resorted to roosting in a tree.

I was very concerned. If he had not

accompanied Rhoda into the barn, he could be anywhere. He had already been the exception to the rule that the cockerel will stay with the hen. His stroll down our track on Sunday had proved that.

I was becoming worried that time with my new cockerel could be quite short.

Headlights shone down the track and my husband's car pulled up at the gate. I explained the situation and was extremely relieved when he immediately began helping me look for my wayward young cockerel. He took his very bright plug in light from the vehicle, attached it to a long electric cable and flicked the switch. Our car park was immediately transformed. As the light was moved around, from side to side, up and down, I frantically hoped that the next sweep of the bright beam would result in Russet being found and it did. "Here he is," Oh thank goodness. I looked up to see Russet, very high up in the branches of a silver birch tree. What a relief.

"He'll be fine there for the night," said my husband, just about to pack things away before trudging to our cottage for a mug of coffee. "Oh no he won't," said I.

We both looked up. There was Russet, perched high on a branch, preening himself. We watched as his beak went along both sides, carefully aligning his feathers. Then a foot would be raised and he'd give it a quick examination before replacing it on the branch. As far as he was concerned, he'd gone to bed. As far as I was concerned, he had not.

There was absolutely nothing I could do to get him down. I could see my husband was in decision making mode... coffee in the cottage, or cockerel raining from the tree. To my relief, ending the reign of this particular cockerel was imminent. I recalled a sentence from one of my many books on Jack Russells.

'If you are not the obvious choice of emperor, your dog will soon ascend the throne.'

I think to a certain extent, the same can be said of cockerels, especially banties. So... how could Russet be brought down to earth... quite literally? My husband went in search of a suitable implement. Russet was quite high up and seemingly oblivious to the scurrying around going on below.

Right — operation raining cockerel was about to commence. Moving around outside in the dark is precarious for me. Another fall and it could easily mean another broken rib. I steadied myself as best I could, holding the fairly large powerful light, trying to keep it focused on my cockerel. Typically, the preferred ladder was in the cottage, waiting to be used to access an attic. The only item to hand was my husband's. platform steps. He picked up the base, turned it vertically and tried to manoeuvre it towards Russet. I tensed as this improvised 'prodder' swayed back and forth, nearing its goal. Russet continued to be oblivious to this activity, examining his feet with great dexterity. Contact was made. With a slightly irritated sounding squawk, Russet returned to earth.

I remembered… shine the light in his face and he'll stay still.

So I did. He did not. He started to walk towards me. I could not afford to fail. Putting the light on the ground and leaning on the fence for support, I reached forward and encircled him with my arms. Success. Our first cuddle. Not exactly as I'd envisaged, but he was safe.

With great relief and satisfaction, I carried Russet over to the barn for bed. Rhoda barely glanced up from her cosy bed of fresh straw. At that moment he was persona non grata. Being abandoned once was bad enough. Twice was humiliating. Poor Rhoda… I did sympathize. Most females would.

I'm hoping that with some guidance and training from me and from Rhoda, my young cockerel will settle down into a happy life here at Puddles and Pals. If at times he wants to fly up into a tree, then so be it. Just as long as he adheres to the daily routine and that includes going into the barn before dark at bedtime.

As he matures, I'm sure my splendiferous Russet will reign supreme here at Puddles and Pals.

Pickle on the Windscreen

Our trips to North Wales with Cadfael and Cider
are always anticipated with great enthusiasm.
Lists made, itineraries prepared, vehicle loaded,
and off we go for great adventures in Snowdonia.
My husband is Welsh, but it is probably me and
the boys who most look forward to our Celtic
expeditions.

For many years my husband and I have travelled to North Wales with the boys, Cadfael and Cider, to spend a week in a rented cottage. We've always visited the same one and I have come to know the lady who owns it quite well. It is situated in a corner of a field on the farm run by her husband and sons. They farm sheep and cattle.

A short walk along the lane from our temporary home and one is walking in Snowdonia National Park. There is a 360-degree panoramic view and it is one of outstanding beauty. The outline of the mountains against the skyline is dramatically sharp. I feel the same love for it every time I return.

The first year we visited, we walked the 100 metres or so onto Snowdonia, passing a derelict larger cottage just before a cattle grid. We stood outside, looking where pieces of stone had fallen away from the building, the dilapidated condition of it all and the piles of fallen rubble. It looked as if it had been three cottages when built and then changed to make one. A pity that it had fallen into such an awful state of disrepair. It would now be a major renovation project for someone, but had such potential.

As we walked with the boys, we chatted about the pros and cons of acquiring a little cottage in North Wales. My husband is Welsh and I love the remote countryside. It did not seem a viable proposition taking everything into account and so for the many years that followed we continued to rent for our holidays with the boys in Wales.

Returning for our second visit, the nearby derelict looking cottage seemed untouched. Taking the boys for their first morning walk in Snowdonia that year, we turned left after crossing the cattle grid and met a man who lived in a rurally situated cottage in the nearby field. Both my husband and I were extremely surprised and shocked to hear that the seemingly abandoned property by the cattle grid was in fact inhabited by a single lady. Apparently, she'd been living in it for some years, which included the year before, when we'd been trying to peer through the grimy windows to see the ruins within. Goodness knows what she'd have thought if we'd been seen. A lucky escape!

From then on, we referred to her as 'Miss Havisham' when talking about her chosen lifestyle and wondering why and how she coped living in virtual isolation in a cottage crying out for renovation. We met her the following year, our third and she seemed a perfectly normal and likeable lady. We learned something about her history but still never really knew why she lived in the property as it was. At least ten years on and her home basically looks the same, apart from a few more pieces of stone no longer part of a wall, but enlarging the pile on the ground. 'Miss Havisham' still seems happy and enjoying life. Something to which most of us aspire.

Our latest visit to North Wales with the boys was a journey into the unknown as far as accommodation was concerned. The little haven we'd frequented for years was no longer our destination. Outside factors had caused us to seek another rural cottage. Recommendation by the original letting agency had resulted in us heading a mile or two further along the winding lane and just beyond the next village. Our first impression was 'oh dear' and we had great concern for the safety of Cadfael and Cider. I will not dwell on the negatives, as they were not the fault of the agency who did their best to recompense.

After breakfast, I would take the boys for a walk along the lane. Uneventful until about the fourth day when my husband decided to accompany us. It proved to be a fortuitous decision. Leaving the cottage and turning right, we proceeded along the narrow lane, me with Cadfael and The Urchin with my husband. For the first couple of minutes all was tranquil then the sound of cattle, but not coming from the ones grazing in the fields bordering the lane. We turned to look and were somewhat alarmed to see a herd of cattle coming up the lane towards us.

I think it is a generally known fact that

walking near cattle with a dog can be very dangerous. ...

Fatalities are not unknown. The worst scenario is cows with calves at foot, as they can attack, seeing the dog as a threat. In that situation it is advisable to let the dog go, but I think many owners would not abandon their precious friend.

On this occasion, we did not see any calves but the situation was not good. The lane was narrow and the 'wall' of approaching cattle was of serious concern. I certainly would not be able to escape by climbing the stone walls edging the narrow lane, as my severe foot injury would prevent any such manoeuvres. A secondary problem was the fact that the stock fencing was topped with barbed wire. Apart from that, cattle in the field on the other side of the wall were coming towards it, presumably to greet their friends. Although the cattle were only ambling along the lane, their pace was constant and faster than ours. They had passed the entrance to our cottage, so we could not retreat back to safety. My husband and I could have stood flat against the stone walls and hoped all would be all right, but that would not help the boys. Luckily Cadfael and Cider were silent, probably a stunned silence, as they watched the advancing threat loom ever nearer, but I felt sure that would soon change.

We could hear frantic shouts from the farmer

as he tried to call them back. There was nothing else he could do, as he had not the pace nor room to get ahead of them. If he walked faster, that would only have driven them on faster. It was all very worrying.

I can only assume that the farmer spoke to his animals a lot and that they knew his voice and understood they were heading in the wrong direction. Their pace slowed, they turned and began ambling back from whence they had come. He had obviously assumed his cattle knew the routine and had done what he probably did on a regular basis... open the gate for them to head off to morning pastures, whilst he brought up the rear, so to speak. On this particular morning things had not gone to plan.

Cadfael had not made any noise when seeing the cattle although looked slightly 'en garde'. His urchin son had adopted a stance of alert concentration and was on the verge of vocal indignation.

Probably we all breathed a sigh of relief as we carried on with our morning walk that sunny Welsh morning.

We like to revisit various old haunts when in North Wales. Having been going to the area for many years we have quite a long list of favoured places. Ruins of once majestic castles, mines going deep underground and the various little steam trains chugging through incredibly beautiful scenery. The boys always come on the trains with us and seem to enjoy looking through the windows of the old carriages as much as we do. On our latest trip to Porthmadog from Blaenau Ffestiniog they were given some dog biccies by a steward. Very tasty, from the way they were happily munching and crunching.

One year, the lady who owned the cottage we'd visited for over a decade had suggested we vsit Yr Ysgwrn, home of the Welsh poet, Hedd Wyn, 1887-1917. We did and were very grateful for the advice.

It was a lovely day as I drove the Welsh roads and we both enjoyed a mug of hot chocolate and a slice of cake in the farmhouse style cafe before going around the old farmhouse, the home of Hedd Wyn. The staff who guided us from room to room so obviously felt the emotion of the story about the son from Trawsfynydd. Indeed, I think all who visited that day and learned about him, also did. If ever in driving distance, I thoroughly recommend anyone to take a couple of hours to go and hear about Hedd Wyn.

My father fought in WW1 and I am regarded as co-author of the book 'Advance and be Recognised', where his words tell of the reality of life as a soldier fighting for King and country and as such, I have learned more than some about

WW1. I found our visit to Yr Ysgwrn, where we learned of the poignant and tragic story of Hedd Wyn, added to the images already in my mind about the traumatic happenings in that war.

We left in sombre mood, but the beauty of the Welsh countryside soon brought us back to cheerfulness as we sped along the roads leading us back to our holiday cottage.

When exploring the various little villages in North Wales, we have found many places that serve wonderful tasty lunches, as well as scones and cakes. We often set a route which takes us near one, so we just have to call in and check if the same high standard is being maintained. Many permit dogs, either outside or inside. So many people visit the area with their pets, that by not allowing canine companions would notably alter the economy.

We popped into a Tourist Information Centre nestling on the edge of one particular village Beddgelert, to ask about the best rural route back towards Betws-y-Coed. There was a very helpful man behind the desk, who was very pleased to assist. A very large and detailed map was on the wall. He pointed out where we were and proceeded to tell us in a very strong Welsh lilt, the way we should go. My husband and I listened intently as he repeated the roads we should take. Yes, we had both heard correctly. We should take the road to Llan Ffestiniog, a few lefts and a right, over the cattle grid then turn left where the garage and cafe used to be. 'Used to be?'

Whenever possible it is I who do the driving. Although I can now face being driven in a car by someone I know, many of the Welsh roads and lanes we travel are far too narrow and winding for me to be a passenger. So, returning to our car, we put the boys in their secured pens and with me in the driving seat, set off. Somewhat surprisingly, the route was remembered and I turned left off the road, opposite nothing − presumably the old site of the garage and cafe no longer there. Driving along the lane, high up in the Welsh hills and mountains we could see for miles. Any car coming from the other direction was visible a long time before we met and so plenty of time for one of us to pull into a passing place. As we sped on our way, I saw an even narrower lane forking off to the left. Things were going so well, that I decided to take the even more scenic route. Grass was growing along the middle of the lane in places and I silently hoped that we were the only ones using this rural route as passing places were in very short supply. Up and down the hills we went, with no other vehicles to be seen. Finally, we reached some sort of civilisation, a few cottages set amidst pines and fields. Cautiously negotiating the many twists and turns, signs to where we wanted to go became visible. We'd made it and included our more rural diversion via Penmachno.

The following morning, we popped into the Tourist Information Centre in Betws. The man behind the counter looked up. "Oh, you made it then. You are not dead."

We recognised the voice and the face. It was the same man who had given us the directions the day before, when in a village the other side of the mountains.

He was right. We had made it and we were not dead.

On our most recent holiday to North Wales — the one with the cow incident — we decided it was definitely the year in which we would try and find a really good beach. The type with miles and miles of soft sand, where we could stroll and the boys have fun and not compete with too many others for a place in the sun. We'd found several beaches over the years, but none were perfect.

Ideally, we wanted to find one with parking places for Blue Badge holders, easy access to the beach and nearby loos. A local cafe selling artisan ice cream within easy reach, would be the cherry on the cake so to speak. So, once again, we visited the Tourist Information Centre at Betws-y-Coed. Another map on the wall scenario with another Welshman pointing out a few beaches and giving us a brief description of each. He too had a very strong Welsh lilt as he told us of the facilities at each. We understood the gist of what he said and decided to visit Harlech.

Many times over the years, the feet and paws of our intrepid little group had walked the pavements in Harlech. The castle is well worth a visit and managed by Cadw, the Welsh equivalent of the National Trust. They run an excellent cafe and sell good quality gifts. The narrow little road leading to the small car park for castle visitors can easily be missed. If entering Harlech and thinking the satnav directions must be wrong yet again, in this instance they are probably correct.

It was only the second day of our holiday and the morning dawned bright and sunny. As it was going to be The Day of the Beach, we decided it would also be The Day of the Picnic. Just before we left for Wales, I'd purchased some individual, open-topped pork pies, from our local farm butcher shop. I am not usually a fan of the pork pie, but none matched the taste and quality of the ones made by this butcher's wife. My diet is limited by my many allergies and so I'd first sampled a tiny piece with trepidation. None of my food allergies are fatal but they can make me feel very unwell. If I had to sum up my allergies in a few words, they would be, 'there is no logic.

So, two little pork pies, encased in crunchy pastry and topped with pickle and a small slice of

Stilton, plus a few other tasty morsels, were put in the picnic basket and the car loaded. Cadfael and Cider would have doggy treats. Bottled water was always on board. I decided to throw caution to the wind and take one of their toys, a longish stick with a cup for a ball on the end. With a swing of an arm the ball leaves the cup and flies through the air with excited dogs in full pursuit. I'd weigh up the pros and cons of using it after seeing if many other canines were visiting Harlech beach that day. I'd sneaked it on board without them seeing, so there would be no Jack Russells demanding 'we want to play now' as we travelled through the Welsh countryside. I know the roads well and have a satnav, but in view of the 2005 crash and my caution of some driving situations, I tend to verbally check the routes with my husband, so am forewarned of any 'iffy' bits. "Is it the one with the cafe and garage that aren't there?" I asked. Affirmation was given It would be the historical coaching route. Miles and miles travelling near mountain ridges and open pastures, lakes — some looking dark and foreboding, others sparkling as the sun shone on the Welsh waters. It is not a route for the faint-hearted. Apart from not going through Penmachno, it was the same one where some years before, the Welshman had pronounced, "You made it, you are not dead then."

As previously explained, I talk to the boys all the time and they were well aware that a special day was about to unfold. They understand so many words and their little faces beamed, eyes glowing with excitement, as we boarded the vehicle which would take us to beach utopia.

There had not been many other cars using our chosen route. I think many tourists like to stick to the main roads, whereas we prefer the uncrowded lanes used by locals. It can make driving a little more stressful in some of the narrow, windy places as locals everywhere have a tendancy to drive fast, feeling that they know the roads so well. That's just the way it is. However I'll stick to the more rural routes, as being part of a line of cars, following exhaust fumes does not fill me with great joy.

About an hour or so after leaving the cottage, we were approaching Harlech. The satnav did not deviate from our usual route to the castle. In fact, we were sent the full distance, taking the narrow road which led to the castle car park. We continued on past, around a few very tight bends until seeing a little sign indicating that we should take a track through the golf course. We bounced along, over the ruts and avoiding the sprinkling of golfers crossing the track in a couple of places. The horizon ahead was mounds of sand dunes with protruding grassy tufts, obscuring any view of beach or sea. Finally, the soft sandy track beneath the wheels changed to solid tarmac as we entered a large parking area off to the right.

There were not many cars parked and several empty spaces for holders of Blue Badges. I reversed into one, turned off the engine and we both sat there looking at the small turnstile gate on the left, over on the other side. A couple of people went through the gate and headed off along the well-trodden sandy path leading up through the sand dunes. They disappeared from sight. There was a small toilet block near to where we had parked. We knew that just opposite Harlech Castle was a little shop which sold wonderful artisan ice creams, so all that was needed now was a lovely sandy beach and then our wish list would be complete. We took the boys out on their extension leads for a wee and poured them a drink, giving thought to our next move. It was about lunch time, so perhaps indulge with a bite to eat before heading off through the gate. Cadfael and Cider were keen to explore but hearing the sound of rustling paper bags, were happy to jump up into the front and sit on my lap whilst my husband rummaged through the basket in the back, searching for tasty things to munch.

He carefully balanced several items in a line along the top of the dashboard, with the pork pies taking pride of place. We had not included such refinements as knives and forks, just a couple of well-travelled picnic plates and a roll of paper towels. I reached for the tub containing snacks for the boys, who by now were bouncing around full of anticipation. Cider was on Neil's lap in the front passenger seat, whilst Cadfael was trying to balance on mine, desperately trying to prevent the steering wheel from blocking his view of the selection of tempting goodies. I decided to have my artisan pork pie. Whilst the pies are classed as individual in size, they are probably just a little too big to allow a bite from top to bottom. However, to avoid too many crumbs, I was determined to try. I leant forward to pick one up, whilst Cadfael fidgeted around, still determined to have full view of the proceedings. I managed to grasp my pie, sat back into the seat and opened my mouth in anticipation. At that precise moment, Cadfael decided he needed a better view. He went to the left, knocking my pork pie to the right before it launched forward like a missile straight onto the windscreen.

"Oh blast," said I.

"What's the matter?" asked my husband, with his head low as he peered into his bag of crisps, searching for a suitable shape. I replied in a somewhat terse voice… "There's pickle on the windscreen."

I wiped off the offending pickle with paper

towels, sat back and ate my pork pie, minus most of the pickle. In the meantime, Cadfael had decided that perching on the handbrake would give him the best view. It was an enjoyable munch. The boys had enjoyed their tasty treats, washed down with another drink. We packed away the remains of the picnic, donned our jackets, attached leads and we were ready to go exploring.

My husband had Cadfael and I had Cider, both Jacks bouncing excitedly up and down as we neared the little grey stone building which was the toilet block. As he diverted in, Cadfael's extension lead handle was passed to me. Cider and I slowly proceeded in the opposite direction, towards the turnstile gate, Cadfael was apparently unaware that control of his lead had changed hands, until he was brought to an abrupt halt, having reached the full extension length.

He is such a handsome dog and he looked magnificent as he stood alert in the middle of the Harlech car park with the sun shining down upon him. If a dog's face can show annoyance, Cadfael's did in the extreme, as he realised that progression towards the gate had ceased. However, he did not have to maintain his pose of indignation for long as a few minutes later, having all manouvered ourselves through the turnstile, twelve feet trudged along the sandy path as we headed off for what we hoped would be our beach utopia.

We reached the end of the sandy path and contemplated the mounds of sand dunes ahead. Not the easiest thing for me to walk on, as the soft giving sand causes me to be at risk of falling. Prevention is better than cure and moving at the fastest speed possible is the safest way for me. The long leads of Cadfael and Cider are attached to my belt, one on either side and as soon as they hear me say the words "Go, go, go", they set off in a forward direction towing me along behind them. They may be small but over the years both have been of considerable help with my walking. I always say that they are "highly trained." My husband laughs at this, but in reality, they are and react to my commands with enthusiasm. Their strength is far more than one would expect and instead of me lurching from side to side, the three of us progress up the incline with great gusto. The way ahead is not that wide but we soon reach a small level area. My husband brings up the rear and as no dogs nor people are on the downward trek, our final push begins. The four of us reach the top of the dunes intact and look in wonder. Beach Utopia does exist.

The tide is out and miles of compact, damp sand spreads out ahead and on both sides. Some distant specks are in fact people, a few with dogs, all enjoying themselves on Harlech Beach.

It may have taken us several years to locate the

perfect beach, but we finally found it in an area which offered everything we wanted. I did consider not naming the actual beach, but it is plenty big enough for us all. If you do visit and hear someone shouting, "Go, go, go," and see two highly trained Jack Russells vigorously helping to pull someone up the sand dune incline, do stop and say, "Hello." Probably best wait until we reach the top though, as their little feet may have difficulty in getting going again over the deep, soft sand.

I will leave details of our beach antics that day for another time as my husband indicated that he'd like to call in at the Golf Clubhouse which was relevant to the golf course, through which the sandy path traversed. Signs were sparse but we finally ended up in a small corner of the car park, beyond which stood The Clubhouse. It was not an imposing building and the boys and I decided to remain in the car as my husband trudged off to ask about green fees. To the non-golfers, 'green fees' is the cost of one round of golf on a course, when not a member of the relevant club. This particular course is a links course, one by the sea. Neil returned, saying the cost for one round was not worth it, being very expensive and from what I understand, a single golfer has to give way to pairs etc. and that is not much fun. Two steps forward, one step back scenario.

We left the area and I drove back up the narrow, winding lane, being pleased to see that one Blue Badge parking space outside Harlech Castle was vacant. Time for a big decision... walk over the road to get an artisan ice cream, or go for a hot choc and a slice of cake and a drink in the castle café. The latter won... and it was lovely.

We always try and return to some of our favourite places. One in particular is in the town of Conwy. Years previously we had visited the old town, primarily to view the castle. Steep and narrow steps led up to the top and whilst I waited below with Cadfael and Cider, my husband made the climb. I am basically used to missing out on a number of things I would like to do, but at times still feel some irritation as to the reason. It would not have changed anything, but an apology from the offending driver who drove his car head on into ours whilst he was on the wrong side of the road, would have helped.

The boys were quite content to remain with me. The paved area was nice and wide, with plenty of room to avoid other people with their dog companions. I heard a shout and on looking up, saw my husband silhouetted against the bright sky. So high up and impossible to recognise but only one person was waving their arms in our direction with calls of Cadfael and Cider drifting down. He reappeared some minutes later and we all moved off towards the old town. Narrow streets, quirky individual shops help make it our kind of place. Feeling a bit peckish, we kept a lookout for something to eat. One particular shop sign seemed to indicate that books were their thing, but as I tried to peer through the misty windows, customers could be seen sitting at tables enjoying refreshments. A little hanging sign indicated that dogs were welcome. So, we negotiated the entrance and manouvered ourselves past the eclectic mix of seating. It was very busy. There were several signs that other dogs were present, as we looked to see if there was any room for us. A tail, a paw, a head — all indicating that canine friends were also enjoying the hospitality offered by this quirky place. There was a lovely ambiance throughout, but we began to think there was no room for us at this particular inn.

Then from a couple seated at a table on the right, came the invitation… "Come and join us." There were two fairly large dogs with them just visible, tucked away towards the back, so I was a little reluctant to accept, knowing how Cadfael can be with other dogs. However, my hesitancy was met with further encouragement to join them, "Plenty of room, come on, come and sit down." Oh well, why not give it a go!

I edged in to one of the two vacant seats, trying

to get Cadfael underneath the table but furthest away from our temporary canine companions, neither of whom had shown any sign of irritation. Due to the general hustle and bustle, Cadfael had apparently not picked up on the fact that he was being steered towards other dogs, which caused me a feeling of extreme relief. My husband managed to get Cider settled and quite remarkably all remained relatively calm... for a while. I think Cadfael felt obliged to make a gesture of Jack Russell supremacy, but after a few growls and fidgeting around, the boys happily crunched on the free dog biscuits offered to all four-legged visitors by cheerful staff.

On the wall opposite, was a large plaque inscribed with wording more or less telling everyone to 'sit down, shove up, get cosy and make room for all.' Well, we'd done that and it was working well.

It was pleasing for me to see that there were several items on the menu which I could safely eat. I chose some 'homemade' soup and it was not long before a steaming cauldron was placed in front of me, together with chunks of crusty brown bread. Lovely! I can't recall what my husband had ordered, but we both thoroughly enjoyed the chosen items. Our table partners had told us they were locals and regularly popped in for a light lunch. They finished their morning refreshments, put on jackets, extricated their two dogs, said goodbye and went on their way. About an hour passed as we enjoyed the food and conviviality of the quirky little place. Several customers, upon seeing Cadfael and Cider sitting on the floor, had come and said "hello" to them, or as Cadfael would interpret it, paid their respects. Rested and with renewed energy, we collected up bags and carefully worked our way towards the door leading to the busy street. This place is definitely one of our favourites.

Various people relate stories of being wet in Wales and whilst the sun has not shined down on us every day throughout our Celtic adventures, the number of rainy days we have had over the past ten years can be counted on fingers. Every time we head to North Wales, 'the Spa bag' is always on board — swimwear and towels, to use when we visit the Spa in Betws-y-Coed due to rain preventing outdoor activities. To date, it has never been unpacked!

As we head home at the end of yet another week treading Welsh ground, I am already planning for our next Celtic trip.

Epilogue

It does not take long to get back into the day to day routine at our little haven in north Herefordshire. My ducks will be happy for me to be back home and the boys will enjoy their usual activities, once more laying claim to the large comfy armchair in our kitchen.

I sometimes wonder if others, returning from a holiday, feel a little sad. Much as I love visiting North Wales, there is always a feeling of anticipation as we finally bounce along the track leading us back. Ducks, dogs and our little cottage, nestling in rural tranquillity, combine to give the feeling that we are coming home.

I hope some of my tales may have caused you to smile and that you have enjoyed reading about my rural lifestyle.

I would like my life of caring for all at our cottage to continue for the foreseeable future. There are definitely further tales for the telling.

The antics of the ducks - Puddles and Pals, the Jack Russell boys — Cadfael and Cider and the chickens, will continue to surprise, amuse and at times, give cause for concern. I so enjoy having such colourful characters in my life. Long may they reign.

Life at ours may be many things, but it will never be dull.